Raw Emotions
Poetry of Life's Experiences
(accompanying artwork)

by Barbara Mitchell
Copyright © 2024
All rights reserved

To Alison, I hope these words inspire & encourage you! Barbara

Acknowledgements

The following poems in this book first appeared in other publications:

Inspiration (Christian Single – 1992)
Solo (With – 1992)
Victory (I Know You Lord – 1994)
Give me the Wisdom (Esprit – 1987)
Winter Miracle (Glad Tidings – 1992)
It Doesn't Seem Possible (Christian Single)
For my Daughter (Parenting Treasures)

These poems were also included in my first poetry publication titled "I Know You Lord"

Dedication

This book is dedicated to Frances Pelletier, my sister and dear friend. We enjoy so many things together – long chats, checking out art stores, thrift shopping, creating art, encouraging each other with all our shows and accomplishments. But I am also so thankful for all her help in fixing, arranging, disassembling, renewing, and teaching me things in the technical world and anywhere I need expertise.
Thank you my sister - for always being here!

Table of Contents

Family/Relationships

For My Daughter	7
Adolescence	8
Alzheimer	9
Never the Pretty One	10
Camped Out	12
Finders Keepers	14
Solo	16
Our Own Manuscript	17
Motherhood	18
Building a Garden	20
Anniversary	21

Nature/Inspirational

Hope	23
Finding the Light	24
Fire Flame	26
Happy in the Crowd	28
Like Copper	29
Perhaps	29
Verbalizing Nature	30
Sand	31
No Expectations	32
After the Burn	33
The Sweetness of Drowning	34
Retirement	36
The Color of Imagination	38
Stand Strong	38
The Wind	40
Happy Voices	41
The Fragile Dance	42
Steps of Living	44
I Am	46
Perseverance	47
Landscape	48
The Ritual of Lighting Small Fires	50
Miracles	52

Table of Contents

Grief and Loss

Absence	54
Hostage	55
Small Tree	56
The Way We Hide	57
Visiting Hours	58
For Leslie	59
I Cannot Resurrect My Loved One	60
Winter in the Garden	62
Boy of Silence	64
Where Have You Gone	66

The Wordsmith/The Artist

Soaking	68
If	69
We Are Not All In Love With Sleep	70
Muse	71
Who Am I	73
We are Poets	74

Spiritual

Winter Miracle	76
When	77
Anchor of Hope	78
Inspiration	79
It Doesn't Seem Possible	80
Give me the Wisdom	82
Holy Comforter	83
With God Between Us	84
Victory	85
Let's Talk about some Poems	87
Let's Talk to the Author	89

Family/Relationships

For My Daughter

I am aware of the child you were
grasping clumsily now
at things that speak of young girlhood
and your eyes though warm for me still
are more often shadowed in dreams
of what is to come
and I know that soon my peace
might well be shattered
in the wake of your goodbyes
as you hurl yourself with full delight
at life's offering

I am aware of the child you were
of the young lady you have become
and I prepare my memories now
for the day
when my arms will not be enough
to keep you here

Adolescence

When my son opens his mouth to speak
everything in the universe
angles its attention
towards the glide of his mouth
And we who waited for days
with starved expectation
for the rumbled sounds
to break free of his throat
who longed for his wandering mood to break
forgive him yesterday's strained silence
overlook the ritual of boredom
that sat like a weight in his eye
We lean into the shifting air
swaddled in the warm mutterings
of his loosened spirit
and the mediocrity of our lives
flares into brilliance

Alzheimer

Mama never knew why the birds came every day
to flock inside her head
why thunder rolled from the tips of their wings
syllables loud behind the eye
she never knew sometimes
who she was
or why

All she knew was flowers
and the peace she found in gardens
how for some short time they freed her mind
as daybreak brought her silence
She lured each frenzied whirl of black
with simple song and subtle craft
called them forth one by one from swirling thought
to feed upon the open hand of morning

Now, Mama no longer finds peace in gardens
Her mind sits at an odd angle
and the birds stay firmly nested in her head
content to feed off slanted thoughts and dream of roses
while my Mama wanders many gardens
forgetting why she came

Never The Pretty One

She dreams of white birds inhabiting her body
their plump forms pushing
beneath the mantle of collarbone
pressing up past sloped shoulders into proud posture
She imagines the cobra, uncoiling itself from sleep
in the slouched cave of her spine
stretching her to a lean line

She has had enough of eyes
shutting down when she walks by
blinking her to a vague impression
furtive glances skipping past her stories
She fears dying in a sluggish life
limping past adventure

She longs to waken in someone else's dream
fluid limbs dancing beneath a wafer of moon
she is keeper of dark mysteries, inflamed secrets
and she prowls the night in search of sacred rhythms

She has had enough of speech that fails her
the oppressed silence
that shudders upward from stifled bones

She longs for voice saturated in fluency
the anointing of rhyme
easy movement of word on word
She wants to steal into life
like an explosion of verse
like a heart's fist turned inward
like a language doubled over
in grief
or laughter

Tonight
she dreams she is woman reborn
a galaxy of beauty pivoting on an axis of grace
she is stunning stars into meteor showers
All eyes turn towards her
and the whole world spins on her image

Camped Out

My son is camped out behind his eyes
secretive and silent
he is fugitive in the center of his forest
Brooding a flame of discontent
he hunches into the heat
tending to his small angers

Latticed against the stubborn dark
he prowls his adolescence
walks his breath in circles
around the vaulted flame
contemplates the fiery shape
of disorder in his life

My son stumbles
through this ceremony of darkness
wrestles sixteen years
that fan up in haze through his eyes
His hands are busy with agitation
as he searches
for some misplaced piece of himself
lost in the disfigurement of past hours

There are no trails leading to his confusion
and I am on the outside of the rim of his trance

How am I supposed to bring him air
close his wounds
How am I supposed to cross this space
volatile now, as dry timber

My son is camped out behind his eyes
and I am on the outside
waiting
for his return

Finders Keepers

We weep for the things we've lost
Small trinkets our mothers gave us
the bookmark that marked her pages
the way we couldn't read
what she was trying to say
Small words that sit like weight between us
The way we wish we'd taken time
to know someone

Our tears fall for the small things
The moment of chance that fell out of a day
because we were too blind to see
The way undone grievances can haunt us
even into the next morning

We look for candlelight, moonlight
Any kind of brilliance to shine out our darkness
reshape them into something pretty
something luminescent
And then one day we are out walking
and there on the ground is a token
a gesture, like a ticket stub to some grand ball
or the remnants of a letter tossed aside

And we read the dear mother in the salutation
or the apologies of hurt
and we slip it into our pocket
along with the broken door key
that we found once on a disorderly path
place it near the antique nail and tiny scissors
we found once in an abandoned sewing kit

We go home and put them in our treasure box
and the sharpness of the scissors reminds us
of things that can wound
So we call up our mothers
and the people we've rushed past
and we cut a new pattern
one we can keep and hold close

And the broken door key says go home
make amends
Take the nail out of your heart
and let yourself bleed
Believe in what you find
take pride in what you keep

Finders keepers
the only way to take someone else's treasure
Find something - and make it your own
Keep something - let it change your life

Solo

I tried to heal myself

I tried to keep the pain inside
sewn up tight behind hasty sutures
but it had a will of its own
and wouldn't be held
oozing out instead
through puckers in the stitching
spilling to the ground around me
until someone dared to stop
dared to question
why closed wounds bleed
and looked a little closer

I tried to heal myself
and found it couldn't be done
alone

Our Own Manuscript

In the world library there are many books
but the two most cherished
carry the names of our children
works of art we created in the sweetest hours
when the whole world was still
and their heartbeat was a murmur between us

We wrote them into a miracle that came to life
and now we carry them in our arms
cradle them carefully so as not to crease their binding
so as to leave their backs unbroken

Everyone stops to read their smiles
grasp at the leaflet of their palms
and we who sit and linger long on the big steps
look down and marvel
that we ever committed such manuscripts to life

Motherhood

There are some who travel to distant shores
where beauty lies in silent pools of emerald green
and silver bursts of moondust thread the stars at night
There are some who roam the sandy dune
to leave their name engraved
in burnished sunlit splendor

But I who never journey far
nor follow adventure's lure
am ever thankful for things I see
for tiny feet that pound their rhythm
round my dreams
and color scenes of everyday
with fleeting magic smiles

There are some who talk with desert men
and hear how harsh winds beat the earth
and whip the barren land
And yet I hear the strangest tales from tiny lips
of gnomes and fairies weaving spells
of wicked things that lurk in homes
and dare to hide beneath the narrow bed

Yes, I who never share
the past of mystic captive kings
nor walk through ancient Aztec tombs
housing ancient dreams
have built within my heart a shrine
of treasures beyond price

of impish grins and dimpled cheeks
tiny hands that bring me gifts
of worms
and rocks
and things

I brave the harshest climate
when tempers are unfurled
shed tears that flow from deep within
they carve ridges in my soul
I watch the radiant dawn burst forth
in love's forgiving smile
while lodged within this heart of mine
lie landmarks of this child

Building a Garden

Yesterday
you brought me flowers
your catcher's mitt a clumsy vase
for yellow stems with lavender blooms
so rare
I knew you'd picked them
from some secret place
it took eleven years to find
and though your eyes
made hasty dodge when meeting mine
I saw the smile curve its way
around your mouth
I saw the way love drifted in
to hang around in silence

Today
I found another bloom, copper-hued
and knew you'd gone some extra step
to place it there
left with care among my favorite things

And though you gently shrugged my hand
and turned instead to pictures on the wall
then taking up your striker's pose
you talk to me of batting scores
and outfield goals

I see the way lives re-arrange
adjust to things we dare not say
I see the way two hearts go on
to build themselves a garden

Anniversary

Thirty years fidget in the air between us

Candlelight cannot camouflage
the vivid glare of our differences
and our words time-worn and frayed
maneuver on the nervous edge of this moment

Your eyes shift to mine like a duty rehearsed
then slide away
Hands embrace the glassed stem
and we mime tradition
while our tongues circle tedium
on the rim of crystal

You and I are the blank stare of old linen
a setting tarnished and dull
Our eyes search the room
for a story we can adopt
to embellish our own meagre union

Thirty years
and the hour lies deflated between us
while all our syllables
leak into empty space

Nature/Inspirational

Hope

Behind this door
lies the ripe fuel of tomorrow
Walk into it or away from it
Discover if the shy twist of a day
can make your breath catch
If the wind can sweep up your words
and bring them home again

Open the door and walk into something quiet
Walk out of it and let your senses
fan out into the universe
Let this doorway be your portal
to shout out accomplishments
to pull in happiness
to learn a new narrative

Let it be the place you walk into
or out of
to illuminate
your true self

Finding the Light

I am on the inside of myself looking out
I am stillness

I go down deep sinking under the layers

I pull up a chair
and listen to the quiet
It surrounds me like a season
That significant, that subtle

I enter my soul and I burn from the heat
I encounter the bloom of myself
and I scribble against the backdrop of the bland
I fall into the essence of the soul's mystery
and I resurrect

I am alive

Finding the Light - Acrylic

Fire Flame

When we dance in our primal goodness
and the wash of the fire flame ignites our spirit
we feel the call of the wild
the pull of the untamed
and we are homing to our soul skin
It is our place of birth
the one that lives inside us
that internal flare
we leave over and over to enter the world
the one we are beckoned to, lured into
But when we come into our calm
and seek deliverance from chaos
we hold out our hands, throw them to the skies
and the fire pulls us in
and every sweet light danced off the flame
enters through the portal of our eye
flies to the heart
and all the days missed
are but a vapor

Fire Flame - Acrylic

Happy in the Crowd

This is where I belong

Dancing a colorful step
through the blanket of greenery
small grass
low grass

The day is completely my own
The sun is a burning sphere in the sky
and I belong to this heat of excitement
a cloak of attention baked onto my skin

The sun adores me
and it funnels its warmth
into every pore of my being

I am brilliant

Like Copper

the pulse of our life
is fluent
movable
everchanging
adapting

                                        Perhaps

                perhaps we do not wish to be resiliant
                            but the circumstance
              we find ourselves in sings in our ear
                                moves us forward
                                one step at a time
                        while we try to decipher
                              where the song
                                      is leading us

Verbalizing Nature

When your world turns upside down
and there are no words to describe
the place you find yourself in
When the familiar becomes unknown
and safety turns to fear
When visiting in numbers comes down to one
And you are talking to yourself
solitary
alone
Always remember you can verbalize nature
Nature is familiar with the shifts you are going through
She has been driven into deep despair
with the fast approaching winds
and the turbulence of storm
With no warning at all she has embarked on journeys
that seem insurmountable, raging fire
the high flood of a river
But when everything has been burnt down
tossed and churned, floated away
then we are left with the burning desire to rebuild
And we can say the words out loud
I managed
I came through the depths, I was challenged
I survived

Sand

This is the true beauty of standing in sand
that the feet so gladly sink into the coarse granules
believing that is what they were made for
the stop-gap between land and sea
And if I moved them outward
and let them curl into the water's sway
small tides lapping at my knees
they would believe that too

That is the grace of leading your body
where it finds its most peaceful state
telling it things until it believes your stories
helping it to forget past landmarks by showing it new ones
The body is malleable
and goes anywhere without complaint

No Expectations

Imagine this is your mind
a clean slate
no interruptions
no debris of the day settling into the crevices
no expectations
no one coming

Imagine this is your mind
solid and solitary
lit with incredible hue
subtle
muted
or as glorious as you wish

Imagine your mind
standing still
no movement
only breath
in and out
stationary
full
regenerating

After the Burn

after the fire
after the broken landscape
and the uprootedness
and the scorched dreams and hollowed out bracken

after the embers burn down
and the sheer desolation stares us in the face
and we tremble on the edge of uncertainty

after
we reclaim and rebuild
and refashion the hurting earth of our lives
then, finally
we come to sit in the afterglow
the rebirth, the new beginning
the stronger rooting and the shared compassion

finally we sit
in the afterglow
of a terrain that anchors us deeper
makes us more resilient out of the ashes
that have scattered
and we can finally recover from the burn

after

The Sweetness of Drowning

I wander blindly to open water
Throw myself at the mercy of its waves
Let them tumble me into a spinning shoreline
After all, blue rivers run the course of my arm

I wear this sweetness of drowning like a brand on my skin
Water pulled up into my lungs
I turn liquid
A mad woman spit up into the ditches of life
I tread the hours with spinning glory
My mouth hungering for the wetness of rain

The Sweetness of Drowning - Acrylic/Resin

Retirement

You don't just start retirement
or begin
You don't just take leisure by the hand
and make it your walking partner
You have to introduce yourself slowly
like a breath
like the smallest flutter of a wing

You have to stand back and observe for a moment
marvel at the uniqueness of it
the gift of it coming to you with open arms
You need to stand still
and wait
take one gentle step until you can call it learning
another step until you can call it familiar

Retirement doesn't just happen
it blooms
like a vibrant blossom that has you
gasping at its beauty
the way in which you will come into yourself
each day
each hour
a moment unlike any other

When you can say
I am comfortable with all this time
I am confident I can fill or not fill each minute

Retirement can be a casualty
or it can be a calm
Ask it its purpose
What is its rhythm
Listen
Be still
Retire in the beauty of the quiet

The Color of Imagination

if being alone colors us bland
and so much stillness makes us blue
and the cycle of solitary leaves us blind
then dip into the color of imagination
swim in the hues
propel yourself through a forest of teal
and drape yourself in the golden fronds of blissful nature
tiptoe your way to magic
and let your eyes open wide

Stand Strong

let adversity bend me
let it coil itself around me
and still I will find a way
to straighten the path I take

if necessary I will fold myself
into strange and beautiful shapes
to survive

The Color of Imagination - Acrylic/Resin

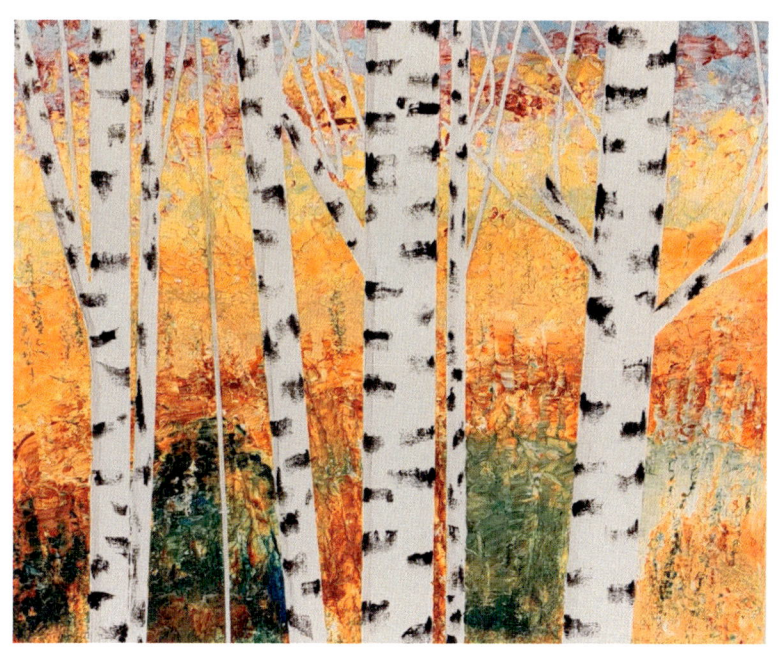

Stand Strong - Acrylic

The Wind

If the wind blows
in a different direction than what you are used to
feel it on your face
hear its whisper
but know that you do not have to follow it
And if the sun breaks through your eyes
and causes you to see something that hurts
that is too sharp for your vision
that is too ripe or not right for your line of thought
then shutter down
and be still

Let the quiet invade your eyelid
let it sink you into its mercy and keep you safe
And if you are walking
and the moon illuminates the path
but it is a path that would lead you away
from what you know to be true of you
then move into the shadow
sit softly in the night's undercurrent
and let it breathe itself into you

Let your direction be still

Happy Voices

When you fill a city with happy voices
it sings and the illumination begins in the underbelly
rising upward through foundations of people's lives
the windows they look out of
the rooftops they raise their eyes towards
and their songs rock the air
and the vibration begins a dance that swirls upward
from door to door
from portal of earth
to portal of heaven
And the skies swim with color
and pour down upon the people
and they are washed in rhythm
a brilliant hue cascading down their arms out of their mouths
into the streets
and they splash and laugh out loud
in their city of happy voices

The Fragile Dance

No matter how weak my spirit
nor how frail my limbs
I will continue to dance the fragile dance

I will not surrender to my moments of low
but always aim for the high in my hour
even if it is small

I will spin on my tiniest breath
move through my pain
I will stepdance my way to renewal

I will applaud myself
in this dance to embrace life

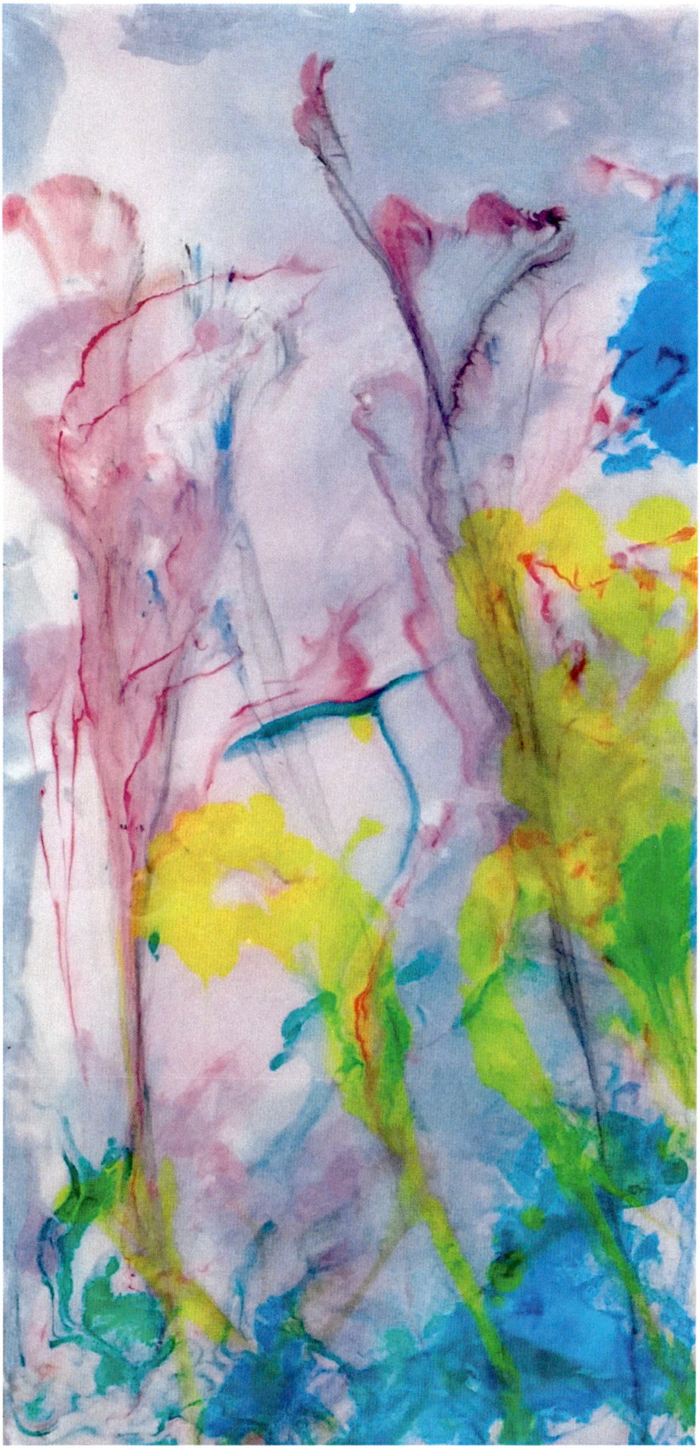

Steps of Living

With every step you take
have a blissful affair with life
Linger over books and poetry
scribble your words on serviettes
let every thought be a bleed on the page

Be spellbound by circumstance
adventure
new faces
but always hold dear the ones you already carry in your heart

Crave family, small children
for they teach you the secret of belonging
Collect experiences
feel every one deeply

Love pizza, fine foods, Thai cuisine, embrace new flavors
enjoy the wonder of appetizers
of nourishment and of life

Walk down lighted avenues
and tell it your innermost thoughts
Be wounded, be vulnerable
be strong
Carry the rhythm of learning within you
let it manifest in your conversation, and your silence

Evolve
rearrange yourself
Grow in your beliefs
be liquid
be light

Trap all good things
to savor for another moment
Aim to be whole
believe in yourself
let it become your second name

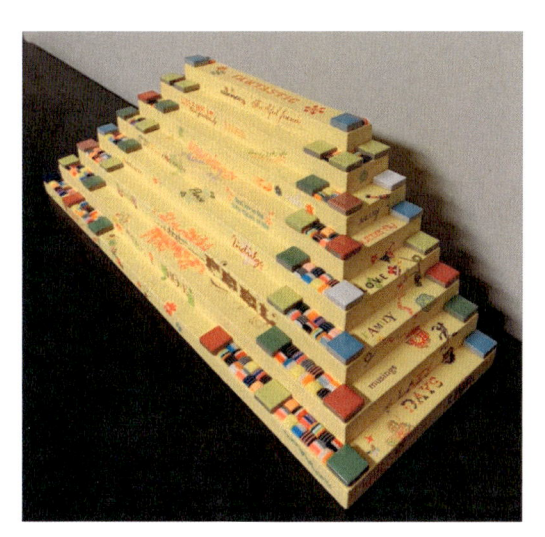

Steps of Living - A Mix Media Project

I Am

I am a sunset gone wild
a disclosure of hot flash and cold winds
a torrent of spinning cycles of storm
I fly parallel to the pull of gravity
and am lulled into shorelines of whimsy

I am a lost girl
in a forest of people's opinions
I am warrior
I tear down branches
tumble through leaves
run my way to sunlight

I will persevere
I embrace the fullness of nature
and it wells up within me
I am wind and rain

Just call me power

Perseverance

I refuse to walk bent and humbled
under the weight of a million moons
Rather, I should brush against the final edge of despair
to be redeemed with hope
to feel the pull of dawn's grey hold
remembering night and dark are day disguised
and watch my dream unfold again
glow bright like burning suns
igniting life
and love

Landscape

there are abrasive walls we lean into
that refine our backbone
the meandering of soft texture
to cradle the hurt

sharp pebbles impart us to step careful
and the smooth round of the stones
soothe the arch of our footstep

we are a landscape being fashioned
from dangerous edges
into mindful certainty
the steel of our spirit honed on rock

we become strong and resilient
we honor the journey it has taken us
to get here

landscape

there are abrasive walls we lean into
that refine our backbone
the meandering of soft texture
to cradle the hurt

sharp pebbles impart us to step careful
and the smooth round of the stones
soothe the arch of our footstep

we are a landscape being fashioned
from dangerous edges
into mindful certainty
the steel of our spirit honed on rock

we become strong and resilient
we honor the journey it has taken us
to get here

barbara mitchell

The Ritual of Lighting Small Fires

Begin with something small, like a flame
Turn it into a habit, a reverence
eavesdrop on its lesson
learn it like you learn yourself
the way you stand vulnerable beneath the circle of sun
and let the truth of its hot center melt into you

Choose another flame, brand yourself in its name
until it burns a warm path through every hard bone
This is the easiest way to come out
on the inside of the heat
Fire has been known to refine a whole forest

Don't back down, take out all the fears you own
reframe them in the light, and the ones that bind you
let them fly away as cinder
the ones that fuel you, tame with your courage

And when you are done with the fears
let your eyes steal into some other piece of blaze
Run your hand over the heat
press it to your soul's need and go deep inside
Lay out every dream that is stillborn
its useless mass lying like a weight
in the hollow of your rib

Weigh it against the odds of use
If it can no longer draw breath, disassemble it
If it it harbors a heartbeat, make it your disciple
teach it to stand upright, persuade it to uphold you

Offer yourself to the language of each amber dance
then see how the prayers line your heart
how close they lean one to the other
so that when one grows weak, another lifts it up

Then take those prayers, fuel them with the fire of belief
and they will ignite, in union, in power
in the passion and the presence
When you are at the center of your burn, feel it
do not be afraid of the clogged breath
the chokehold it has on you
sink into its awkward arms, let it grip you
inhale it, live it
become

in its dance to your soul, it wants to own you
and forever after
sun circles will round out your vision
a stab of warm heat will burn in your hand
and the fever
will keep you alive

Miracles

I stand breathless in the midst of young miracles
     tiny hands throw love around my knees
     and squeals of their singing spirits
     flush my day to fullness
            with vagrant hearts
            they are spinning on freedom
            stealing secrets and scenes from the hills
            pocketing life with mischievous glee

I grow weary in the midst of these miracles
     for they are losing themselves in the range of cloud
     content to drift on a whim
            with eager faces caught up in a laugh
            they are snatching up wind
            in the white of their teeth
            while I am left tangled
            in flurry and fleece

I am helpless in the midst of these miracles
     for they have grown tall
     and their long limbs lean into the swath of tomorrow
            they have loosened their stride
            and their eyes revel in the vision
            of distant dreams
            while stretched between us
            lies the grand goodbye...

Grief and Loss

Absence

Where have you gone
that I can no longer find you
into what silence do you turn and hide
that my words come back to me thin with despair
If I reach for you, you become like mist
and my hand cannot hold you
Your eyes once fluent with luminous glow
are now but a pooling of shallow light
they have turned to still waters
with no familiar current to draw my smile
Where have you gone
that I am left with only this dark hour
to unravel my longing
Where have you gone
that even the flowers of your hand
no longer grow up through the slats of mine
and this heart is a dry meadow
aching
for rain

Hostage

When you are not here
the whole house aches
The walls that stood at attention
droop and sag
leaning into the corners
and the floors take on a tilted posture
their polished surface folding into themselves

Windows shutter out the sun's glare
and the doors lock themselves
the jamb of their despair
angling across the threshold
Even the keys lose their place

The whole house is taken hostage
by your absence

Small Tree

Your death
was like good earth breaking
heaving in on itself
The once vibrant soil a betrayal to its keeper
like the vibrancy of your skin and heart
a traitor to your namesake

Your life
collapsed
causing a huge fissure in my own life
calling me to fall into my own decline
But like your last breath
that called me to stay strong, to stand firm
so it was that I laid down roots in your dying
planted myself in the sorrow of your leaving

Now, I am a small tree
growing, seeking sunlight and clear air
and somewhere always with me
your life force secures me
holds me upright

The Way We Hide

All hell breaks loose
when I am carrying the apocalypse in my pocket
The tremors start small in the base of my hand
like an earthquake seizing up for a good split

I tremble only slightly
while I pretend the earth might not break in half
taking me with it
and all the suns in my eye shut down

It's the dark that holds me so fiercely
the blank slate of spinning into all that black
and the scream of everything that lives inside

Still...I adhere to the belief
that all things need to be broken
to be made whole again
and so I allow the shifting to occur
I cannot breathe but I learn to encourage
the lack of rhythm in my body
I cannot think but I learn
to look forward to the emptiness in my mind
I cannot move but I learn to be a pillar of quiet
No one sees the turmoil inside

I am breathtaking in my pursuit of containment

Visiting Hours

We have built our marriage
on the childish rhythm of tiny feet
whirling past our silence
        have been thrilled
        with the rush of sudden laughter
        that fires a room with invisible glow

We have built memories
on dissension hurled at a glance
borne our failures loudly
        heaving them off the shoulder
        of matrimonial stability
        willing them into something salvageable
        to measure against the scale of maturity

We have carved the remembrance of sorrow
 into soothing echoes
that offer us healing
        and even now in your despairing pain
        with tubes and bars between us
        we are building memories
        the dry parchment of our hands clinging in love
        to the final chant of sleep's eternal charm

Even now to the end
we are building

For Leslie

My dear high school and long-time friend
who passed away from Lou Gehrig's Disease 2017

This chair might hold me hostage
and my physical self be limited
but remember to look me in the eye
Inside I am a whirl of color, a rainbow of huge proportion
flooding the world with light

Remember to ask me how I am

I may be a quieter journey now
but still a journey nonetheless
leaping over obstacles and embracing conversations

Remember to celebrate with me
the laughs and the love
for I am a turnstile of heaping emotions
and I have many words glued to the back of my throat

Remember to sit with me
take my hand, for you are all still dear to me
and I would hold you if I could

Remember to look at me
for I am still here

I Cannot Resurrect My Loved One

I cannot resurrect my loved one
No manner of speech
no attempt at bartering will bring him back

Pleading with the universe
beseeching the big quiet, does not return him to me

So instead I rob our family albums
line up photographs
dozens of them scattered across
the length of the floors
I weave them down the hallway
make a map in the image of you
cross reference you with my memories
underline you with a tear, a laugh

I light candles
lay out the treats you used to love
across the counters
shuffle your baseball cards
organize your hockey albums

I sit in your favorite chair
imagine you reading the paper, a novel
a poem you wrote me

I take out the small tape recorder
listen to the songs I tucked into your ear
at the hospice

I wear your shoes, a sweater you gave me
I dig out your rings
twirl them on the palm of my hand
carry them in my pocket
sleep with them under my pillow

I say your name out loud over and over
I listen for you
I hear you laughing, making a joke
making me angry
making me smile

I cannot resurrect you
bring you back
but I always carry you inside my heart

I always remember you

Winter in the Garden

In this season when your heart bleeds its prayer
and your soul is silent in its god-sense
When you sit in the heaving hollow of this day's hunger
and stillness and peace is the cushion you ache for
remember that I am waiting on the far side of the garden

I am a spinning center of whispering words
and though I dance a snowy circle inside the gate
do not think I forget you
for while I scatter the freshness of my spirit
to the throbbing winds and my footsteps dance a pattern
in the glistening white
remember
it is you I dance for
It is for you I wear my reverence

I turn you in the easy caricature of my heart
and with every note of my singing
I am lifting you to the heavens the way
the dying blades of grass beneath the white, lift their heads

I search out every hidden miracle
in the corner of this garden
and paste them behind my eyes
to bring to you later, as gifts

Do not think I forget you
for I am witness to the glory of this season
and I will bring you communion
in the simple flow of scripture
that will move
from my breath
to yours

Winter in the Garden - Encaustic

Boy of Silence

In the beginning there was my son
a ceremony of such small proportion
he arrived in a swath of silence
I waited for his song, but his voice
was a trapped bird in the throat
He grew to a pale shadow, eyes smudged to neutral
he filtered my comings and goings in half tones

I copied the form of my lips over and over
against his ear
but his teeth clamped tight
against the easy slur of speech
He never came out of his silence
leaned instead to the quieter syllable
that scribbled its reason inside his head

I prayed for transparency
for his skin to thin to a clear hue
a window to see what passed for words
through his blood
I waited for understanding
to learn why he traced his hearing against mirrors
laid his face flat against windows
Perhaps he felt small in the midst of such big hours
soothed himself
by finding definition against reflection

Perhaps the world was too noisy for him
He huddled, one leg bent up and over the other
sometimes he curled backwards
The contortions he went through, to find peace

He would sit for hours
take part in the sun's departure
watch its round face a brilliant wound
slip over the edge of the earth
and all movements of him were still
His eyes fixed
I am sure he bears the scar of every sundown

In the end there is only my son
and all my grief sharpened to love
A pulse of joy flares in his heart and his eyes
unbutton to the glory of a new dawn
Even as he pulls a sigh from the ordinary day
he is reaching for me
teaching me to celebrate
in the space between words
He dances through hours, his lips a pressed secret
brightness curved to a mood that swings inside him
Maybe a music maker resides in his limbs
for he spins and sways
hands braiding the air, themselves
they swipe at laughter dangling in open space
I'm sure I see it enter his face

In the end there is only my son
and with our hands joined
together we are fluent
in our composure of silence

Where Have You Gone

Where have you gone
to what horizon have your feet fled

This garden grows thick and my prayer wheel is gone
covered over by brambles and leaves
and the spirit of God I used to carry so easily
has confounded me

I turn my face to the sun but it shies away
hiding behind dark clouds that sit like sentries
over the garden path

I am waiting still, at the gate
but the broken hinge hints at time passing by
and my leaning has become as rusty as the latch

The catechism of our time is torn out page by page
and I watch them flutter helplessly in the wind
My hands snag only air

I have lit the path with tea lights
am burning incense to invoke the help of bored saints
with little else to do except turn their attention
to lost loves

I wring my hands
calling out to a God I still try to believe in
and I chant
I don't want to forget you
I don't want to forget you

The Wordsmith/The Artist

Soaking

You can soak in the spirit of anything…

The sunset bending itself backwards over the horizon…the day sneaking up on the dawn.

You can soak in a voice, in a song…a rhythm can pull you in and you can drown in its meter and rhyme.

You can lose yourself in the midst of a single minute, you can come undone at the crude arrangement of words hurled in anger. You can soak in all the hurt and astonishment that goes with it and write it out as your history.

You can soak in love and pull its vibrancy around you…you can learn the inside of a dream if you sit with it long enough.

Soaking urges you to look in the corners of conversation and pull something out for yourself…or you can give something back.

Soaking in the spirit is your way to freedom…the path that leads you to yourself…and out again. It is to immerse yourself in the divine, the disabled, the disorder, the despair…it is soaking and sinking and rising up clean.

If

If I could begin again
I would paint my sidewalks blue
I would put paper flowers in my garden
so that when I needed blooms
I could mount them on my walls

I would breathe in sweet music
and exhale notes we have never heard before
I would be a queen or a pauper
wear finery or threads
just to see what it's like

I would run on the inside of clocks
and learn time in a different way
I would be more of me and less of others

My spirit would run unleashed
and only the fairy dust from magic
could corral it

Then I would be a sparkling wonder
spinning on the spot
dancing in a pot of paint

We Are Not All In Love With Sleep

The clock ticks away the hours
under the dark ceiling of night
I toss and turn thinking of the gospel of color
the scripture of teal blues and dancing pastels
I see the minutes creeping around the numbered face
and the drone of wasted time is too much for me

I leap from my bed
I am twirling down the stairs
conversing with my brushes

I read myself into the pale white of the canvas
punctuate the night with the flood of sunlight yellow
and burgeoning pinks

I stamp my feet in the dripping drops
of dylusion inks
and I am a happy mess of art gone wild

We are not all in love with sleep

Muse

I am the muse and I am the art

I am a watercolor
breathing new rhythm
scripting new territory
with the stroke of my brush

It bleeds crimson
from the caved hollow inside my rib
stains the soul's pocket stitched to my heart
I lure dusty black crows from the clouds of my eye
and they haunt their dark frenzy into my hands
as I pound the night into ink
with the wildness of their muse

With my hand upraised let the hue anoint me
let the cobalt and fuscia spill down my arms
let every good resin stain my teeth

I am the gaping pigment of a sky blown wide open
the smoking dust of a fired gun
a pale reed strangling on a flow of emotion

I am ancient rhythm rooted in texture
a flurry of whitewash

I brush myself alive

Imagine This! - Alcohol Ink

Who Am I

Yesterday thinks I am the shy wind
the soft breeze without description
the hushed whisper you never hear

Today thinks I am a busier element
the frenzied torrent, a cyclone of disorder
Tomorrow thinks I am an accomplished weather artist
I can be anything I like

But I am not what time thinks I am
I am nothing elemental
I am no one's dust storm
nor anybody's whirlwind

I am poet
writer
inventor of words
and I always stay indoors

We are Poets

we are poets
starving ourselves to a thin shape
on a diet of measured words

    we could write novels plump with delicacies
    fatten the page
    but we don't wish to be that large

        buffets of fiction beckon
        but we shun the verbal trough
        stark truth is what keeps us narrow

but in the night when no one sees
we hoard buttery words, layer them on the page
succulent, they tempt us with their full phrases

    then we remember
    we are poets
    we want our bones lean, the frame delicate

        so we rid ourselves of the excess
        weigh the syllables, trim the edges
        till only the tracings
        of how we wish to appear
        remain

Spiritual

Winter Miracle

walk with me into this miracle
where the dazzling white fires of winter fields
burn the eyes
and the sieving of crystal ashes through our fingertips
ministers healing

come, take my hand
and we will venture where frosted limbs lean
without fear into the wind
where the pale hands of trees beckon to embrace us
where coolness rests on our shoulder

we will sink into the weight of their compassion
and our prayers of thanksgiving
will soar like blazing embers

sit beside me
and we will discern together how God renders to us
these miracles of contradiction

we will feel for ourselves
how His blessings rise from the depths of the cool
yet settle like Spring in the heart

we will feel for ourselves
what it is
to discover this miracle

When

When my green hope withers in the gathering dust
and its faintest stirrings shrivel in the sobbing wind
When apathy invades this sluggish spirit
and my drowsy will sinks into the soft bed of despair
It is then You come to me
with the grace of dawn
bending me to a new beginning

You show me you are the soul of the earth
and its very heartbeat throbs to your Holy pulse
With mighty hands
You lift me from corrupt soil
choke out the deadroot
until cultivated in the perfection of Your light
I rise up, once again
trellised in Your goodness

Anchor of Hope

Are there times it seems the pain in your heart
Swells like the restless tide
When all around is turbulent sea
And the shore is never in sight

Are there times it seems the sky is dark
And storm clouds threaten above
You're filled with despair and your hope-flame dies
And help from your friend is not enough

It's at times like these when life's cresting waves
Threaten to drown and destroy
That God pulls out His anchor of Hope
And pulls you safely to shore

Inspiration

It wasn't from cresting the vaulted depths
    with the height of the climb at my feet
It wasn't despairing to see more terrain
    that caused me to fall in defeat
But surely when softness cushioned my walk
    apathy echoed its song
For I plodded the barren stretch of routine
    with no challenge to spur me on

It was never the turbulent waters
    that raged and tore through my life
That left me floundering, helpless
    adrift in the surging tide
But rather the lulling beauty
    and the lure of familiar shores
That fashioned my days with indifferent thought
    and compelled me to stay where I was

So Father, give me a yearning
    for the valleys shadowed and steep
For deserts that breathe their fire and dust
    for waves that crash at my feet
And surely then I'll accomplish much
    when stirred by the spiritual pace
When inspiration is fueled on the path
    of hardship tempered with grace

It Doesn't Seem Possible

It doesn't seem possible, Lord
that this is the way You would have me go

My feet were not fashioned to tread
the hot parchment of desert
and my temperament did not approve
of such fiery attentions
I sought only rain, yet when it did not come
I found my roots securely anchored
in a land that was once my enemy
and my footsteps carried the patterning of scrolled sands

I took no comfort in hard soil for my bed
yet I learned to adapt to the contours of earth
Rock became my companion and I saw how one discovers
the miracle of cored secrets hidden away
by chipping away at the stone

I stood mute and weary before the mountain's grandeur
and despair overcame me
yet I found a strength that comes from within
and I learned how weathering serves to shape
rather than defeat
how sharp edges are smoothed away with elements of time

I was never prepared for ice that thawed beneath my feet
yet I learned to read hope in the swirling undertow
and perseverance became my preserver

No, this was never the way I would have chosen
but then You knew that didn't you
and You chose for me

Give me the Wisdom

Give me the wisdom, Lord
not to question
why the days have passed so long and dark
nor to seek an answer
to yesterday's pain

Let me give no thought
to what tomorrow brings
lest despair reach out to drag me down
and my soul's flame flicker and dim

But rather, give me patience
to accept what was
and is
That the rhythm of Your leading
might be sufficient guide
that all the fears I harbor
might be less
because You hold them in Your hand

Holy Comforter

You have moved into me
quietly
carefully
Spooled across my thoughts with delicate maneuvers
ladled your warmth into the palm of my hand
You have held me speechless
with the pooling of psalms at my feet
prismed me in the light of Your laughter

You have entered into my place of holy
graced the altar of my heart with God's flame
burning bright in your eye
gathered ashes from the hearth of my pain
and scattered them wide to retreating wind

You have moved into me
so quietly
so carefully
when the black hour comes
and I lean into the dark
I can hear you breathing
beneath my skin

With God Between Us

With God between us
we will tread careful through the burning edge
of each other's pain
place our footprints side by side
and with cautious steps
steal across the blackened earth
that lies beneath our feet

With sacred hands to hold
we will dare to gather the branches of self
and sift through hurts braised by Satan's flame
With delicate maneuvers
pare away the weakened bark
to chance it with our caring in hopes of resurrecting
these greening shoots of worth and veneration

We will step wisely through paths corrupt
and though the ashes of reflection
rise up to clog our breath
we will glean a purer air
in our search for fresher soil

We will tread careful
with God between us
and once again know a land
that is good to itself
and its people

Victory

I no longer offer strains of fear to starving seasons
and the taste of anxious days has left my lips
for I savor a new and sweeter song

Though the winds of winters past
sharpen their anger on my doorpost
and the howling tempest prowls
beneath my window to seek his entry
I grant no invitation and shun his seeping fury

For I have the blazing fires of Holy Words
on which to warm my hands
and Your heat rises to shield me
I bend to stoke the heartened embers
and Divine Light flares in my eyes

My voice exults in heavenly praise
and the icy shoulder of destruction
steals away
to swallow its own devouring song
and feed
on meagre silence

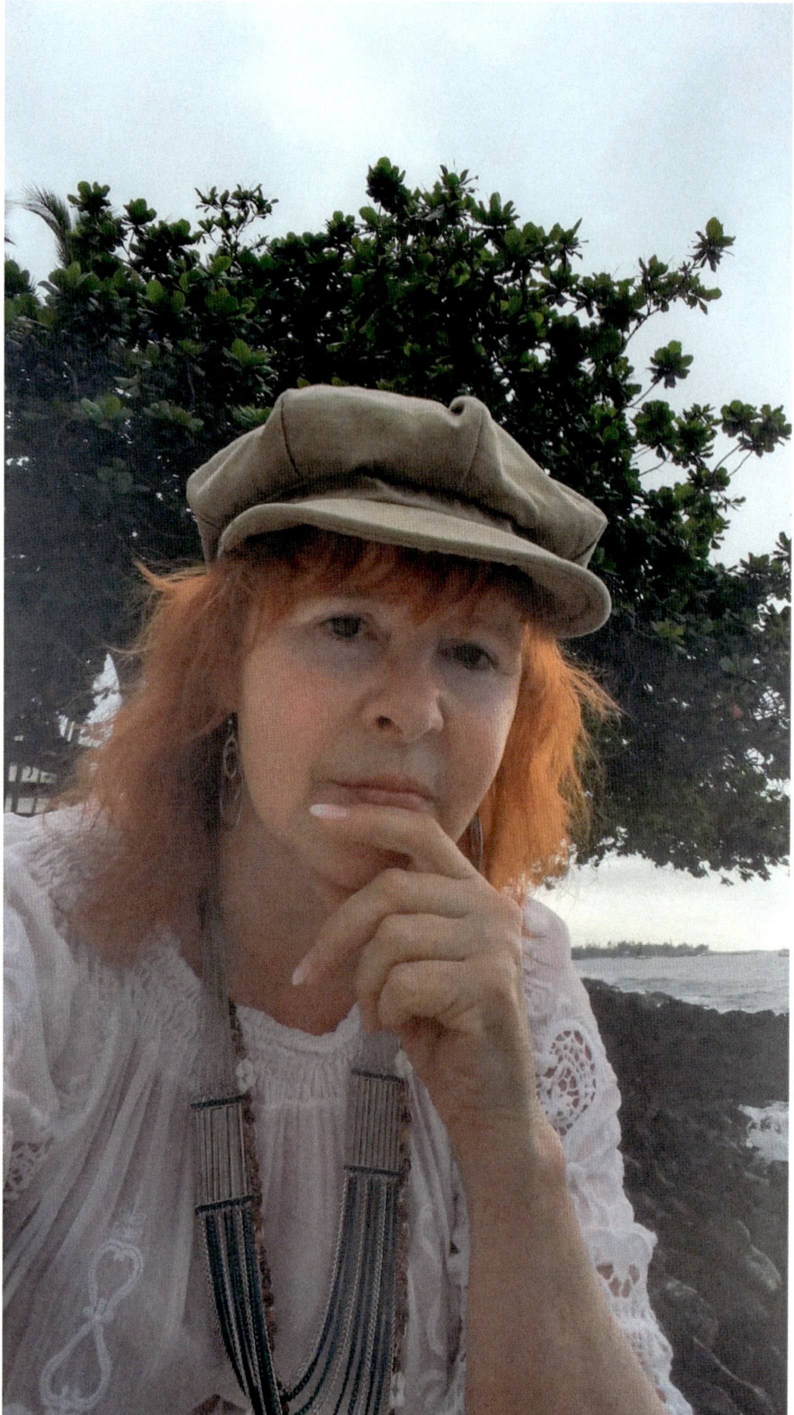

Let's Talk About Some Poems

Some of these poems were written during our long season of Covid and the quietness which entered all of our lives. We were forced to remain solitary and a good way to make sense of it all, was for me to put down on paper some of the things I was feeling.

It was rejuvenating to discover that stillness can be a godsend, leaving us in a place of the alone. I didn't so much find that the physical quietening down was a surprise, as much as I found the quietness of the mind to be.

I embrace a lot of energy and can physically, have busy days, so yes, it was nice to have no demands, appointments, callings, meetings, etc. But to find the mind at a total standstill, was unexpected. If our lives are more still, then there is less activity and organization happening in the mind. I treasured this.

I painted 40 paintings in the first two months, as I had no idea Covid would go on as long as it did, and so initially, I wanted to utilize my quiet time while I had it. I also wrote poems to go with all the paintings. Some of the paintings are also included in this book.

Poems that came out of this impacted time.
- Finding the Light
- The Fragile Dance
- Stand Strong
- No Expectations
- Happy Voices
- Steps of Living
- Happy in the Crowd
- If
- The Color of Imagination
- Hope
- Verbalizing Nature

Let's Talk to the Author

I first became interested in writing poetry around grade four, but the crux of my interest arrived during Junior High School. Perhaps what appealed to me most was the way it helped me to sort through the emotions and angst that teens can go through and gave me an outlet to share some of those feelings with friends in a nonthreatening way.

When a poem was accepted for publication in my high school years, in the international Teen Magazine, I felt elated. I think it gave me the encouragement I needed apart from my family's enthusiasm for my writing.

Getting married in 1978 and raising two young children took me temporarily away from poetry, but by June 30, 1985 I was totally involved in words again when I won an Honorable Mention for a short story submitted to the ACWF (Alberta Christian Writer's Fellowship) annual contest. I joined their writer's group and participated in many different writing conferences for years to come.

Beginning with my first credit in Esprit magazine in 1986 and continuing for the next 10 years, my poetry and stories were published over 320 times in publications in North America and around the world and I had the great pleasure of winning poetry contests through various outlets. This did not come easily, but rather from the continuous and ongoing support from many people who believed in me and helped me take the steps necessary to make myself a better and more articulate writer.

One great experience was seeing my first poetry book published in 1994, (I Know You Lord) and also my poetry translated into Braille for distribution by the John Milton Society for the blind. My poems have also been distributed in Eastern Europe after translation into a variety of other languages.

The other great experience was being a part of WISP (Writers In School Program). I was invited to various schools and presented customized creative writing workshops to grades 1 through 9. In some, I integrated poetry with the art of collage as a method of teaching children self-expression.

Now, many years later, I am still writing and incorporating much of my words into collage and mix media artworks. There is nothing quite so fine as dancing in a pot of paint and mixing it with metaphors of life.

Manufactured by Amazon.ca
Bolton, ON